CLASSIC C

C000142213

CLASSIC COMFORT

Timeless Wisdom
from Classic Writers

Compiled by Robert Backhouse

Hodder & Stoughton
LONDON SYDNEY AUCKLAND

Copyright © 1995 by Robert Backhouse.

First published in Great Britain 1995.

10 9 8 7 6 5 4 3 2 1

British Library Cataloguing in Publication Data
A record for this book is available from the British Library

ISBN 0 340 63050 7

Designed and typeset by Watermark, Norfolk

Printed and bound in Great Britain by
Cox & Wyman Ltd, Reading, Berks.

Hodder and Stoughton Ltd
A Division of Hodder Headline PLC
338 Euston Road
London NW1 3BH

Contents

Introduction

Listening to the words 'Comfort ye, comfort ye my people' as they are sung in Handel's Messiah never fail to move and sober me. We are all too well aware of the many millions of people who are crying out for comfort. It may take the form of a desperate search for the next meal, or for someone to hug them, or for someone to talk to about an intensely personal inner wound. We are surrounded by the homeless, the handicapped, the unemployed and the abused. People daily endure so many different kinds of suffering and pain – physical, mental, emotional and spiritual. Some pain, like the loss of a loved one, threatens to overwhelm us. It is one thing to know about people who need comfort, but how can we show real compassion?

Once when the apostle Paul was deeply upset, he says that God comforted him. How, we may wonder, did this super-spiritual giant receive God's comfort? Was it through a revelation given by the Holy Spirit, or a mindblowing vision? Was it during a night of prayer or from meditating on the scriptures? God did use all these ways to encourage Paul, but on this particular occasion Paul says God comforted him '. . . by the coming of Titus' (see 2 Corinthians 7:2–7). God comforted Paul through a friend.

Many of us long to be comforters as well as to be comforted ourselves and the best way to do that is to experience God's comfort at first hand. This book collects advice from past centuries about how to pass comfort on to others as well as how to receive it.

Classic Comfort includes extracts from many of the great Christian classic writers who have been revered through the centuries, and whose timeless wisdom is being sought afresh today. Some of these men and women, from a wide variety of countries and Christian traditions, are regarded as saints. None of them is included merely because he or she is a known 'name', but because what was written even hundreds of years ago still brings comfort to our hearts and minds today. Read here words of comfort from the Book of Common Prayer, loving letters to bereaved and troubled friends from Archbishop Fénelon and the hymn-writer John Newton, St Augustine on the mystery of suffering and John Donne's famous sonnet on death. These are just a few examples of the rich heritage left by generations of Christian writers, a vital source of comfort and inspiration to draw on today.

Robert Backhouse
Norwich 1995

PART ONE

THE GOD OF ALL COMFORT

Praise be to the God and Father of our Lord Jesus Christ,
the Father of compassion and the God of all comfort,
who comforts us in all our troubles.
(2 Corinthians 1:3–4)

The God of all comfort

That great teacher St Paul says in his epistle, 'Praise be to the God and Father of our Lord Jesus Christ, the Father of compassion and the God of all comfort, who comforts us in all our troubles' (2 Corinthians 1:3–4).

Three kinds of trouble may fall on a man and plunge him into distress. First, harm to his external possessions; next, to his dearest friends; lastly, shame, hardship, physical pain and distress of mind to himself.

Everything that is not God has in itself a natural bitterness, discomfort and unhappiness. It does not make for the good which is of God and is the same as God, but lessens, dims and hides the sweetness, joy and comfort that God gives.

And further, all sorrow comes from love of those things of which loss deprives us. If I mind the loss of outward things it is a certain sign that I am fond of outward things and really love sorrow and discomfort. Is it to be wondered at that I am unhappy when I like discomfort and unhappiness; when my heart seeks and my mind gives to creatures the good that is God's own? I turn towards creatures, from which there naturally comes all discomfort, and turn my back on the natural source of happiness and comfort. No wonder that I am gloomy and wretched! The fact is, it is quite impossible for God or anyone to bring true comfort to a man who looks for it in creatures. But the one who loves only God in creatures, and creatures in God only, that man finds real and true and equal comfort everywhere.

Meister Eckhart, *Sermons*

The Twenty-Third Psalm

The God of love my shepherd is,
And he that doth me feed:
While he is mine, and I am his,
What can I want or need?

He leads me to the tender grass,
Where I both feed and rest;
Then to the streams that gently pass:
In both I have the best.

Or if I stray, he doth convert,
And bring my mind in frame:
And all this not for my desert,
But for his holy name.

Yea, in death's shady, black abode
Well may I walk, not fear:
For thou art with me, and thy rod
To guide, thy staff to bear.

George Herbert

I bind unto myself today

I bind unto myself today
The power of God to hold and lead,
His eye to watch, his might to stay,
His ear to hearken to my need.
The wisdom of my God to teach,
His hand to guide, his shield to ward;
The word of God to give me speech,
His heavenly host to be my guard.

Christ be with me, Christ within me,
Christ behind me, Christ before me,
Christ beside me, Christ to win me,
Christ to comfort and restore me.

Christ beneath me, Christ above me,
Christ in quiet, Christ in danger,
Christ in hearts of all who love me,
Christ in mouth of friend and stranger.

St Patrick's Breastplate, translated by C. F. Alexander

Resting in God

You are great, O Lord, and greatly to be praised; great is your power, and your wisdom infinite. Yet would man praise you; he, but a particle of your creation. You awake us to delight in your praise; for you made us for yourself, and our heart is restless, until it rests in you.

St Augustine, *Confessions*

Peace

Let the hands or the head be at labour, the heart ought nevertheless to rest in God.

Jakob Boehme, *The Way to Christ*

Comfort is to be found only in God

Whatever I can desire, or conceive, essential to my comfort, cannot be provided by this world, so I look for it in the world to come. If all the comforts of life were within my reach, and I could enjoy all its delights, I could not enjoy them long.

Your complete consolation and perfect delight, therefore, O my soul, are to be found only in God, the comforter of the poor, and the exalter of the humble. Wait a little while, O my soul, wait for the accomplishment of the divine promise, and you shall enjoy the plenitude of good in heaven. By too inordinate a pursuit of earthly good, you lose what is heavenly and infinite. Use temporal things: desire those which are eternal.

The Imitation of Christ, ascribed to Thomas à Kempis

St Teresa's bookmark

Let nothing disturb thee,
Nothing affright thee;
All things are passing –
God never changeth.
Patient endurance
Attaineth all things.
Who God possesseth
In nothing is wanting,
Alone God sufficeth.

St Teresa of Avila, *Poems*

Merged into God's will

To the quiet mind all things are possible. What is the quiet mind? A quiet mind is one which nothing weighs on, nothing worries, which, free from ties and from all self-seeking, is wholly merged into the will of God and dead to its own.

Meister Eckhart, *Sermons*

Lasting comfort

In everything we think of or do, let us take note of divine love. Let us pay less attention to the love of knowledge or argument. Love delights the soul. Love sweetens the conscience. Love draws back from lesser pleasures that allure, and from longings for personal success. Knowledge without love contributes nothing to eternal salvation. Instead, it inflates the wretched self till one bursts open.

Be wise, then, in the wisdom not of this world, but in that of heaven. Be strong in taking on hard labour for God. Yearn to be enlightened with eternal wisdom; be inflamed with fire of sweet love and desire for your soul's Creator, the fire that feeds contempt for all transitory things.

Things that do not last cannot bring comfort. The soul has here no dwelling-place. Restlessly it cries out for the home not made with hands: 'Christ to me is life: to die is great gain' (Philippians 1:21).

Richard Rolle, *The Fire of Love*

PART TWO

SPIRITUAL CONFLICTS

*Our struggle is not against flesh and blood,
but against rulers, against the authorities,
against the powers of this dark world
and against the spiritual forces of evil
in the heavenly realms.
(Ephesians 6:12)*

Dryness

Note one wonderful blessing from the night of dryness. It is in this dark night that the words of the prophet Isaiah are fulfilled, 'your light will rise in the darkness, and your night will become like the noonday' (Isaiah 58:10). When God gives light to the soul, he not only makes it aware of its own miserable state before God, but God also makes the soul aware of his greatness and excellence. God not only dries up the desires and appetites of the senses, he also cleanses the soul and opens the soul's mind to understand the truth.

Delight and pleasure even in spiritual things can cloud and impede the spirit, and what is more, times of dryness of the senses shed light and bring understanding. Times of trouble give us a correct estimation of how empty and naked the soul is, and how much it needs God's power. It is through this dark and dry night of contemplation that the soul is supernaturally instructed in his divine wisdom. This teaching God never gave to those enjoying their initial spiritual blessings.

St John of the Cross, *The Dark Night of the Soul*

Comfort in temptation

Letter to Mrs G. (June, 1777)

My Dear Madam,

Temptations may be compared to the wind, which, when it has ceased raging from one point, after a short calm, frequently renews its violence from another quarter. The Lord silenced Satan's former assaults against you, but he is permitted to try you again another way. Be of good courage, Madam; wait upon the Lord, and the present storm shall likewise subside in good time. You have an infallible pilot, and are embarked in a boat against which the winds and waves cannot prevail. You may be tossed about, and think yourself in apparent jeopardy; but sink you shall not, except the promises and faithfulness of God can fail.

Upon the attentive consideration of your complaint, it seems to me to amount only to this, that though the Lord has done great things for you, he has not yet brought you to a state of dependence on himself, nor released you from that impossibility, which all his people feel, of doing anything without him. And is this indeed a matter of complaint? Is it not every way better, more for his glory, and more suited to keep us mindful of our obligations to him, and in the event more for our safety, that we should be reduced to a happy necessity of receiving daily out of his fulness, than to be set up with something of a stock of wisdom, power, and goodness of our own?

John Newton, *Cardiphonia*

Resisting temptation

As long as we continue in this world, we cannot possibly be free from tribulation and temptation. Therefore, everyone should be alert to the temptations that are peculiar to him. He should persevere in watchfulness and prayer, as his enemy the devil prowls around like a roaring lion looking for someone to devour (1 Peter 5:8). No one, no matter how perfect and holy, is exempt from occasional temptation. Temptation is the inevitable lot of mortality.

But temptations, however dangerous and afflicting, are highly beneficial; because under their discipline, we are humbled, purified, and instructed. All the followers of Christ have gone through many hardships to enter the kingdom of God (see Acts 14:22). There is no order of men, however holy, nor any place, however secret, where temptations and trials do not intrude.

The Imitation of Christ, ascribed to Thomas à Kempis

Falling into temptation

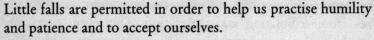

Little falls are permitted in order to help us practise humility and patience and to accept ourselves.
Charles de Foucauld, *Meditations*

Our falls are far more useful to us than victories that are spoiled by vain complacency.
Charles de Foucauld, *Meditations*

Overcoming temptation

Resist the Devil, and he will run away from you.

James 4:7, GNB

When a good man is afflicted, tempted, or troubled with evil thoughts, then he understands better the great need he has of God, without whom he perceives he can do nothing that is good. . . . Yet we must be watchful, especially in the beginning of the temptation; for the enemy is then more easily overcome, if he is not allowed to enter the door of our hearts, but is resisted at his first knock at the gate. . . . For first there comes to the mind a mere thought of evil, then a strong imagination of it, afterwards delight, and an evil inclination, and then consent.

The Imitation of Christ, ascribed to Thomas à Kempis

The devil tempts that he may ruin; God tests that he may crown.

St Ambrose, *On the Faith*

No temptation has seized you except what is common to man. And God is faithful; he will not let you be tempted beyond what you can bear. But when you are tempted, he will also provide a way out so that you can stand up under it.

1 Corinthians 10:13

'Unanswered' prayer

All who call on God in true faith, earnestly from the heart, will certainly be heard, and will receive what they have asked and desired, although not in the hour or in the measure, or the very thing which they ask; yet they will obtain something greater and more glorious than they had dared to ask.

Martin Luther, *Table Talk*

Faith and prayer

I tell you the truth, if you have faith as small as a mustard seed, you can say to this mountain, 'Move from here to there' and it will move. Nothing will be impossible for you.

Matthew 17:20–1

Praise God

Man's chief work is the praise of God.
St Augustine, *Confessions*

Prayer is my chief work, by it I carry on all else.
William Law, *A Serious Call to a Devout and Holy Life*

He who does not praise God while here on earth shall in eternity be dumb.
John of Ruysbroeck, *The Spiritual Espousals*

Dark seasons

Letter to Rev P. (January 11, 1777)

Dear Sir,

Sensible comforts are desirable, and we must be sad when they do not come to us. But I believe there may be a real exercise of faith and growth in grace, when our sensible feelings are faint and low. A soul may be in as thriving a state when thirsting, seeking, and mourning after the Lord, as when actually rejoicing in him – as much in earnest when fighting in the valley, as when singing upon the mount.

Dark seasons afford the surest and strongest manifestations of the power of faith. To hold fast the word of promise, to maintain a hatred of sin, to go on steadfastly in the path of duty, in defiance both of the frowns and smiles of the world, when we have but little comfort, is a more certain evidence of grace, than a thousand things which we may do or forbear when our spirits are warm and lively.

I have seen many who have been upon the whole but uneven walkers, though at times they have seemed to enjoy, at least have talked of great comforts. I have seen others for the most part complain of much darkness and coldness, who have been remarkably humble, tender, and exemplary in their spirit and conduct. Surely were I to choose my lot, it should be with the latter.

John Newton, *Cardiphonia*

Armed for the battle

Be strong in the Lord and in his mighty power.

Put on the full armour of God so that you can take your stand against the devil's schemes.

For our struggle is not against flesh and blood, but against the rulers, against the authorities, against the powers of this dark world and against the spiritual forces of evil in the heavenly realms.

Therefore put on the full armour of God, so that when the day of evil comes, you may be able to stand your ground, after you have done everything, to stand.

Stand firm then, with the belt of truth buckled round your waist, with the breastplate of righteousness in place, and with your feet fitted with readiness that comes from the gospel of peace.

In addition to all this, take up the shield of faith, with which you can extinguish all the flaming arrows of the evil one.

Take the helmet of salvation and the sword of the Spirit, which is the word of God.

And pray in the Spirit on all occasions with all kinds of prayers and requests.

With this in mind, be alert and always keep on praying for all the saints.

Ephesians 6:10–18

The comfort of the 'Comfortable words'

Hear what comfortable words our Saviour Christ saith unto all that truly turn to him.

Come unto me all that travail and are heavy laden, and I will refresh you. *St Matthew* 11:28.

So God loved the world, that he gave his only-begotten Son, to the end that all that believe in him should not perish, but have everlasting life. *St John* 3:16.

Here also what Saint Paul saith.

This is a true saying, and worthy of all men to be received, that Christ Jesus came into the world to save sinners. 1 *Timothy* 1:15.

Here also what Saint John saith.

If any man sin, we have an Advocate with the Father, Jesus Christ the righteous; and he is the propitiation for our sins. 1 *John* 2:1.

The Book of Common Prayer

Unexpected comfort

I asked God for strength that I might achieve;
I was made weak that I might learn humbly to obey.

I asked for help that I might do greater things;
I was given infirmity that I might do better things.

I asked for riches that I might be happy;
I was given poverty that I might be wise.

I asked for all things that I might enjoy life;
I was given life that I might enjoy all things.

I was given nothing that I asked for;
But everything that I had hoped for.

Despite myself, my prayers were answered;
I am among all men most richly blessed.

Unknown author

The comfort of prayer

To focus on the goodness of God is the highest form of prayer, and God's goodness comes down to meet us at our most basic need. It gives life to the soul and makes it live and grow in grace and virtue. God's goodness is closest to our human nature, and the most ready to bring us to grace. It is that same grace which we seek now and will always seek until we know for certain that our God has completely enfolded us in himself.

Lady Julian of Norwich, *Revelations of Divine Love*

He who has learned to pray, has learned the greatest secret of a happy and holy life.

William Law, *A Serious Call to a Devout and Holy Life*

True happiness

If any one would tell you the shortest, surest way to all happiness and all perfection, he must tell you to make it a rule to yourself to thank and praise God for everything that happens to you. For it is certain that whatever calamity happens to you, if you thank and praise God for it, you turn it into a blessing. Could you, therefore, work miracles, you could not do more for yourself than by his thankful spirit; for it heals with a word speaking, and turns all that it touches into happiness.

William Law, *A Serious Call to a Devout and Holy Life*

Amazing grace!

Amazing grace! how sweet the sound
That saved a wretch like me;
I once was lost, but now am found;
Was blind, but now I see.

'Twas grace that taught my heart to fear,
And grace my fears relieved;
How precious did that grace appear,
The hour I first believed!

Through many dangers, toils and snares
I have already come:
'Tis grace that brought me safe thus far,
And grace will lead me home.

John Newton

PART THREE

COMFORTING OTHERS

*Filled with compassion, Jesus
reached out his hand
and touched [the leper].
(Mark 1:41)*

Serving others

Let everyone lovingly cast all their thoughts and cares, and their sins too, as it were, on the will of God. Moreover, if a person, while busy in this lofty inner work, were called by some duty in the providence of God to cease therefrom, and cook a broth for some sick person, or any other such service, he should forsake such work, and go out to preach or aught else, I should go cheerfully, believing not only that God would be with me, but that he would vouchsafe me it may be even greater grace and blessing in that external work undertaken out of true love in the service of my neighbour, than I should perhaps receive in my season of loftiest contemplation.

Johann Tauler, *Sermons*

It is in this life alone we can learn lessons of patience and self-denial; for there are no sick-beds to watch by, no sufferers to comfort, in the mansions of the Father's house.

George Macdonald, *The Kingdom of the Lovers of God*

A reservoir or a canal?

If you are wise you will show yourself rather as a reservoir than as a canal. For a canal spreads abroad the water it receives, but a reservoir waits until it is filled before overflowing and thus communicates without loss to itself its superabundant water.
St Bernard of Clairvaux, *The Song of Songs*

Difficult people

It is no great matter to associate with the good and gentle, for this is naturally pleasing to all, and every one willingly enjoyeth peace, and loveth those best that agree with him. But to be able to live peaceably with hard and perverse people, or with the disorderly, or with people who go against us, is a great grace, and a most commendable and manly thing.

Thomas à Kempis, *Rules*

Bear with the defects of others

The person who bears and suffers evils with meekness and silence, is the sum of a Christian life.

God is the first object of our love. Its next office is to bear the defects of others. And we shall begin the practice of this amid our own household.

We should chiefly exercise our love towards those who most shock either our way of thinking, or our frame of mind, our knowledge, or the desire we have that others should be as virtuous as we wish to be ourselves.

John Wesley, *A Plain Man's Guide to Holiness*

During a long life I have proved that not one kind word ever spoken, not one kind deed ever done, but sooner or later returned to bless the giver and become a chain binding ever with golden threads to the throne of God.

The seventh Earl of Shaftesbury

Speak from the heart

We should speak candidly and trustfully and really be in love with the doctrine we are trying to teach and get people to accept; the great art is to be art-less. The kindling power of our words must not come from outward show but from within, not from oratory but straight from the heart. Try as hard as you like, but in the end only the language of the heart can ever reach another heart while mere words, as they slip from your tongue, do not get past your listener's ear.

St François de Sales, *Introduction to the Devout Life*

Last words

Comfort the poor, protect and shelter the weak, and with all thy might, right that which is wrong. Then shall the Lord love thee, and God himself shall be thy great reward.

Alfred the Great's last words

Patience

How poor are they who have not patience!
What wound did ever heal but by degrees?

William Shakespeare, *The Passionate Pilgrim*

A daily retreat

As the birds have nests on the trees that they may have a retreat when they need it, so our hearts ought to seek out and choose some place each day near to our Lord, that they may make their retreat on all occasions.

St François de Sales, *Introduction to the Devout Life*

PART FOUR

TROUBLES

*For in the day of trouble
he will keep me safe in his dwelling.
(Psalm 27:5)*

Proofs of God's love

One of the greatest proofs of God's love to those who love him is to send them afflictions with grace to bear them.

Even in the greatest afflictions, we ought to testify to God, that, in receiving them from his hand, we feel pleasure in the midst of pain, from being afflicted by him who loves us and whom we love.

The most rapid way which God takes to draw a man to himself is to afflict him in that he loves most, and with good reason, and to cause this affliction to arise from some good action done with a single eye, because nothing can more clearly show him the emptiness of what is most lovely and desirable in the world.

John Wesley, *Christian Perfection*

Man's extremity is God's opportunity.

Anonymous

Troubles without remedy

Take courage, and turn your troubles, which are without remedy, into material for spiritual progress. Often turn to the Lord, who is watching you, poor frail little being as you are, amid your labours and distractions. He sends you help, and blesses your affliction. This thought should enable you to bear your troubles patiently and gently, for love of him who only allows you to be tried for your own good.

Raise your heart continually to God, seek his aid, and let the foundation stone of your consolation be your happiness in being his. All vexations and annoyances will be comparatively unimportant while you know that you have such a Friend, such a Stay, such a Refuge. May God be ever in your heart.

St François de Sales, *Introduction to the Devout Life*

Whatever troubles come on you, of mind, body, or estate, from within or from without, from chance or from intent, from friends or foes – whatever your trouble be, though you be lonely, O children of a heavenly Father, be not afraid!

Cardinal Newman, *Tract for the Times*

Be still in trouble

Be still and cool in thy own mind and spirit from thy own thoughts, and then thou wilt feel the principle of God, to turn thy mind to the Lord God, from whom life comes; whereby thou mayest receive his strength, and power to allay all blustering storms and tempests. That is it which works up into patience, into innocency, into soberness, into stillness, into stayedness, into quietness, up to God with his power.

Therefore be still awhile from thy own thoughts, searching, seeking, desires, and imaginations, and be stayed in the principle of God in thee, that it may raise thy mind up to God, and stay it upon God; and thou wilt find strength from him, and find him to be a God at hand, a present help in time of trouble and need.

George Fox, *Journal*

Indifference to events

Accustom yourself to much calmness and an indifference to events.

Madame Guyon, *A Short and Easy Method of Prayer*

Peace

Renounce desire, and you shall find peace.

The Imitation of Christ, ascribed to Thomas à Kempis

One day at a time

He who has so many reasons for joy, and such great ones, is very much in love with sorrow and peevishness, who loses all these pleasures, and chooses to sit down upon his little handful of thorns. Enjoy the blessings of this day, if God sends them; and the evils of it bear patiently and sweetly: for this day is only ours, we are dead to yesterday, and we are not yet born to the morrow. But if we look abroad, and bring into one day's thoughts the evil of many, certain and uncertain, what will be and what will never be, our load will be as intolerable as it is unreasonable. . . .

Jeremy Taylor, *Holy Living and Holy Dying*

The God who brings the lonely home.

Psalm 68:6, Moffatt translation

Disappointment

Receive every inward and outward trouble, every disappointment, pain, uneasiness, temptation, darkness, and desolation, with both thy hands, as a true opportunity and blessed occasion of dying to self, and entering into a fuller fellowship with thy self-denying, suffering Saviour. Look at no inward or outward trouble in any other view; reject every other thought about it; and then every kind of trial and distress will become the blessed day of thy prosperity. That state is best, which exercises the highest faith in, and fullest resignation to God.

William Law, *A Serious Call to a Devout and Holy Life*

We cannot always be doing a great work, but we can always be doing something that belongs to our condition. To be silent, to suffer, to pray when we cannot act, is acceptable to God. A disappointment, a contradiction, a harsh word, an annoyance, a wrong received and endured as in his presence, is worth more than a long prayer; and we do not lose time if we bear its loss with gentleness and patience, provided the loss was inevitable, and was not caused by our own fault.

François Fénelon, *Christian Perfection*

Disheartened

Should we feel at times disheartened and discouraged, a confiding thought, a simple movement of heart towards God will renew our powers. Whatever he may demand of us, he will give us at the moment the strength and the courage we need.

It is not the multitude of hard duties, it is not constraint and contention that advance us in our Christian course. On the contrary, it is the yielding of our wills without restriction and without choice, to tread cheerfully every day in the path in which Providence leads us, to seek nothing, to be discouraged by nothing, to see our duty in the present moment, to trust all else without reserve to the will and power of God.

François Fénelon, *Christian Perfection*

Do not let your hearts be troubled. Trust in God; trust also in me.

John 14:1

Troubles and spiritual progress

Take courage, and turn your troubles, which are without remedy, into material for spiritual progress.

Often turn to our Lord, who is watching you, poor frail being as you are, amid your labours and distractions.

He sends you help, and blesses your affliction.

This thought should enable you to bear your troubles patiently and gently, for love of him who only allows you to be tried for your own good.

Raise your heart continually to God, seek his aid, and let the foundation stone of your consolation be your happiness in being his.

All vexations and annoyances will be comparatively unimportant while you know that you have such a Friend, such a Stay, such a Refuge.

May God be ever in your heart.

St François de Sales, *Introduction to a Devout Life*

Affliction

My God, I read this day,
That planted Paradise was not so firm
As was and is thy floating Ark; whose stay
And anchor thou art only, to confirm
And strengthen it in every age,
When waves do rise, and tempests rage.

At first we lived in pleasure;
Thine own delights thou didst to us impart:
When we grew wanton, thou didst use displeasure
To make us thine: yet that we might not part,
As we at first did board with thee,
Now thou wouldst taste our misery.

There is but joy and grief;
If either will convert us, we are thine:
Some angels used the first; if our relief
Take up the second, then thy double line
And several baits in either kind
Furnish thy table to thy mind.

Affliction then is ours;
We are the trees, whom shaking fastens more,
While blustering winds destroy the wanton bowers,
And ruffle all their curious knots and store.
My God, so temper joy and woe,
That thy bright beams may tame thy bow.

George Herbert

PART FIVE

ANXIETY

Cast all your anxiety on him [God]
because he cares for you.
(1 Peter 5:7)

Past, present and future

Trust the past to God's mercy, the present to his love, and the future to his providence.
St Augustine, *Confessions*

Time belongs to God

Jesus, by his Godhead, is maker and giver of time. He by his manhood is the truest heeder of time and he by his Godhead and manhood is the truest judge and asker of account of the spending of time.
The Cloud of Unknowing

Change

Do not look forward to the changes and chances of this life in fear; rather look to them with full hope that, as they rise, God, whose you are, will deliver you out of them. He has kept you up to now. Do you but hold fast to his dear hand, and he will lead you safely through all things; and, when you cannot stand, he will bear you in his arms. Do not look forward to what may happen tomorrow. Our Father will either shield you from suffering, or he will give you strength to bear it.

St François de Sales, *Introduction to a Devout Life*

Think only of the present

Let us think only of the present, and not even permit our minds to wander with curiosity into the future. This future is not yet ours; perhaps it never will be. It is exposing ourselves to temptation to wish to anticipate God, and to prepare ourselves for things which he may not destine for us. If such things should come to pass, he will give us light and strength according to the need.

Why should we desire to meet difficulties prematurely, when we have neither strength nor light as yet provided for them? Let us give heed to the present, whose duties are pressing; it is fidelity to the present which prepares us for fidelity in the future.

François Fénelon, *Christian Perfection*

The present moment

God makes of ALL things mysteries and sacraments of love.
Charles de Foucauld, *Meditations*

Why should not every moment of our lives be a sort of communion with divine love?
Charles de Foucauld, *Meditations*

We must cut off all more distant views, we must confine ourselves to the duty of the present moment, without thinking of what preceded it or what will follow it.
Charles de Foucauld, *Meditations*

Try not to let apprehension about the future or regret about the past flood over into your present living and make you miserable.
Charles de Foucauld, *Meditations*

Accepting God's will

Accept his will entirely, and never suppose that you could serve him in any other way. You can never serve him well, except in the way he chooses. Supposing that you were never to be set free from such trials, what would you do? You would say to God, 'I am Thine – if my trials are acceptable to Thee, give me more and more.'

I have full confidence that this is what you would say, and then you would not think more of it – at any rate, you would not be anxious. Well, do the same now. Make friends with your trials, as though you were always to live together; and you will see that when you cease to take thought for your own deliverance, God will take thought for you; and when you cease to help yourself eagerly, he will help you.

St François de Sales, *Introduction to a Devout Life*

Anxiety about tomorrow

He who believes in God
is not careful for the morrow,
but labours joyfully
and with a full heart.
'For he giveth his beloved,
as in sleep' [Psalm 127:2].
They must work and watch,
yet never be careful and anxious,
but commit all to him,
and live in serene tranquillity;
with a quiet heart,
as one who sleeps safely and quietly.
Martin Luther, *Table Talk*

Anxiety does not empty tomorrow of its sorrow – only today
of its strength.
C. H. Spurgeon, *Sermons*

Look at the birds of the air

[Jesus said,] 'Look at the birds of the air; they do not sow or reap or store away in barns, and yet your heavenly Father feeds them. Are you not much more valuable than they? Who of you by worrying can add a single hour to his life?

'And why do you worry about clothes? See how the lilies of the field grow. They do not labour or spin. Yet I tell you that not even Solomon in all his splendour was dressed like one of these. If that is how God clothes the grass of the field, which is here today and tomorrow is thrown into the fire, will he not much more clothe you, O you of little faith?'

Matthew 6:26–30

Consider

Consider
The lilies of the field whose bloom is brief:
We are as they;
Like them we fade away,
As doth a leaf.

Consider
The sparrows of the air of small account;
Our God doth view
Whether they fall or mount,
He guards us too.

Consider
The lilies do neither spin nor toil,
Yet are most fair:
What profits all this care
And all this toil?

Consider
The birds that have no barn nor harvest-weeks;
God gives them food:
Much more our Father seeks
To do us good.
Christina G. Rossetti

Our eternal home

O God, our help in ages past,
Our hope for years to come,
Our shelter from the stormy blast,
And our eternal home;

Under the shadow of thy throne
Thy saints have dwelt secure;
Sufficient is thine arm alone,
And our defence is sure.

Before the hills in order stood,
Or earth received her frame,
From everlasting thou art God,
To endless years the same.

A thousand ages in thy sight
Are like an evening gone,
Short as the watch that ends the night
Before the rising sun.

Time, like an ever-rolling stream,
Bears all its sons away;
They fly forgotten, as a dream
Dies at the opening day.

O God, our help in ages past,
Our hope for years to come,
Be thou our guard while troubles last,
And our eternal home.

Isaac Watts

PART SIX

ILLNESS AND PAIN

My grace is sufficient for you,
for my power is made perfect in weakness.
(2 Corinthians 12:9)

The cross gives us God

God gives the cross, and the cross gives us God.

We may be certain that there will be inner spiritual progress whenever the cross is embraced. Abandonment and the cross go hand in hand.

As soon as anything like suffering comes to you, and you find yourself resenting it, give yourself over to God at once. Commit the suffering to God and offer yourself up as a sacrifice to him. Then you will discover that when the cross does come it will not be such a burden as you had imagined, because you had prepared your heart and mind to receive it.

However, this does not prevent you from feeling its weight, as some people have supposed. When we do not feel the cross, we do not suffer at all. An openness to suffering constitutes a principal part of the sufferings themselves. Jesus Christ himself was willing to suffer the excruciating pain of the cross. We often bear the cross of Jesus when we feel weak, while at other times, we bear the suffering of the cross with fortitude. Both of these experiences should be the same for us, as they are both equally the will of God.

Madame Guyon, *A Short and Easy Method of Prayer*

Without some sorrow and pain no man may live in love.
The Imitation of Christ, ascribed to Thomas à Kempis

Patience in suffering

Dear Madame, (November 12th, 1692)
The only correct course of action for you to take is to bear your cross patiently. The things which are now trying you, which you believe are coming between you and God, will prove to be the means by which you are united to him, provided that you bear them humbly. Those things which overwhelm us and upset our pride do us more good than all the things which inspire us. You, more than most other people, need to be overwhelmed by God as St Paul was at Damascus (see Acts 22:4–11).

Madame, you need to realise that you have no resource in yourself. The deeper the wound is, the more painful the healing will be. Everything that you are suffering comes from God's hand. He is healing you of a wound which you did not even know you had and which is a thousand times more serious than any natural ailment. Pride is more revolting than any abscess although you are not so horrified by it.

Do not be discouraged. Give yourself up into God's hands. He is dealing with you mercifully. God loves you and he wants you to love him just as our Lord did when he died on the cross. If you put no limit on what you expect from God it will be given you according to your faith.

François Fénelon, *Letters*

He who has learnt to suffer

Some people are at peace in their own hearts and live in peace with everybody around them. Some people have no peace themselves and go around disturbing everybody else's peace. They torment other people, but torment themselves even more.

There are some people who not only have peace themselves but make it their business to restore peace to others. After all the highest kind of peace we can attain in this miserable life is made up of humble and patient suffering rather than an absence of adversities. The person who has learnt to suffer the most will certainly possess the greatest amount of peace. He is the conqueror of himself, the lord of the world, the friend of Christ, and the heir of heaven.

The Imitation of Christ, ascribed to Thomas à Kempis

Submit to God in suffering.
Turn it as thou wilt,
thou must give thyself to suffer what is appointed thee.
But if we did that,
God would bear us up at all times
in all our sorrows and troubles,
and God would lay His shoulder under our burdens,
and help us to bear them.
For if, with a cheerful courage,
we submitted ourselves to God,
no suffering would be unbearable.

Johann Tauler, *Sermons*

Pain is my refreshing

I have chosen pain for my refreshing. Therefore it is not hard for me to suffer pain, but rather it is a delight as it is for the love of my Saviour. I will continue to delight in my pain for as long as it pleases his Majesty that I should suffer.

St Catherine of Siena, *Dialogo*

Patience in sickness

For the love of God discipline your body and soul alike, keeping fit and healthy. If you should become ill, through circumstances beyond your control, bear it patiently and wait patiently upon God's mercy. That is all you need to do. It is true to say that patience in sickness and other forms of trouble pleases God much more than any splendid devotion that you might show in health.

The Cloud of Unknowing

The advantages of afflictions

Letter to Mrs S. (December, 1776)

My Dear Madam,

The advantages of afflictions, when the Lord is pleased to employ them for the good of his people, are many and great. Permit me to mention a few of them; and the Lord grant that we may all find those blessed ends answered to ourselves, by the trials he is pleased to appoint us.

Afflictions quicken us to prayer. It is a pity it should be so; but experience testifies, that a long course of ease and prosperity, without painful changes, has an unhappy tendency to make us cold and formal in our secret worship; but troubles rouse our spirits, and constrain us to call upon the Lord in good earnest, when we feel a need of that help which we only can have from him.

They are useful, and to a degree necessary, to keep alive in us the conviction of the vanity and unsatisfying nature of the present world, and all its enjoyments; to remind us that this is not our rest, and to call our thoughts upwards, where our true treasure is, and where our conversation ought to be. When things go as we want them to our hearts are too prone to say, It is good to be here.

Thus the Lord, by pain, sickness, and disappointments, by breaking our cisterns, and withering our gourds, weakens our attachment to this world, and makes the thought of quitting it more familiar and more desirable.

John Newton, *Cardiphonia*

The benefits of trials

To a spiritual disciple (1563)

Learn how to benefit from your sorrows, for they bring great riches to the soul. They cleanse it from past sin; what fire is to gold, tribulation is to the righteous person, whose heart it purifies.

Trials only injure the wicked, for instead of being grateful to God they murmur against him. Their punishment does them no good, because they turn their sufferings into sins, and so lose where they might have gained. . . .

Do not imitate them, but let your courage increase with your trials. God proves his sons by sorrow, and no one will be crowned except for the person who has been through the combat. St James says, 'Blessed is the man who perseveres under trial, because when he has stood the test, he will receive the crown of life that God has promised to those who love him' (James 1:12). If only we realised the value of this crown, how gladly we would now suffer affliction.

John of Avila, *Letters*

Learning from suffering

Sometimes it takes a painful experience to make us change our ways.

Proverbs 20:30, GNB

If God had told me some time ago that he was about to make me happy as I could be in this world, and then had told me that he should begin by crippling me in arm or limb, and removing me from all my usual sources of enjoyment, I should have thought it a very strange mode of accomplishing his purpose. And yet, how is his wisdom manifested even in this! For if you should see a man shut up in a closed room, idolising a set of lamps and rejoicing in their light, and you wished to make him truly happy, you would begin by blowing out all his lamps, and then throwing open the shutter to let in the light of heaven.

Samuel Rutherford, *Letters*

Peace and prayer in suffering

If you can just hold your peace and suffer, you will without doubt see help from the Lord.

The Imitation of Christ, ascribed to Thomas à Kempis

Either he will shield you from suffering or he will give you unfailing strength to bear it. Be at peace, then, and put aside all anxious thoughts and imaginings.

St François de Sales, *Introduction to a Devout Life*

I beg you to cultivate your inner spirit, as this gradually results in everything becoming prayer in you. You will not be free of suffering, but a peaceful suffering is twice as easy to bear as suffering in turmoil.

François Fénelon, *Christian Perfection*

Mental illness

I was a stricken deer, that left the herd
Long since; with many an arrow deep infixt
My panting side was charg'd, when I withdrew
To seek a tranquil death in distant shades.
There was I found by one who had himself
Been hurt by th'archers. In his side he bore,
And in his hands and feet, the cruel scars.
With gentle force soliciting the darts,
He drew them forth, and heal'd, and bade me live.
Since then, with few associates, in remote
And silent woods, I wander, far from those
My former partners of the peopled scene;
With few associates, and not wishing more.

William Cowper (in his mental illness)

Seek God at Calvary

Be patient in all the sufferings which God is pleased to send you. If your love of God is wholehearted you will seek him as much at Calvary as at Mount Tabor and you will definitely find that God's love towards you is even greater.

Don't be like those who give themselves to God some of the time only to withdraw themselves from him at other times. They are only interested in being embraced by arms of love and shrink back from the hands that have been crucified. These people also turn away from divine consolation and prefer human comfort.

No, beloved souls, you will not find consolation in anything except in the love of the cross, and in total abandonment. Jesus made this clear in his rebuke of Peter: 'You do not have in mind the things of God, but the things of men' (Matthew 16:23).

It is impossible to love God without loving the cross; and a heart that delights in the cross, finds the most bitter things sweet. A famished soul finds bitter things sweet because she finds herself as hungry for God as she is for the cross.

Madame Guyon, *A Short and Easy Method of Prayer*

The mystery of suffering

There is no sea so deep as these thoughts of God, who makes the wicked to flourish and the good to be afflicted – nothing so profound, nothing so deep; and in that deep, in that profundity, every unbelieving soul is wrecked. Dost thou wish to cross this deep? Move not away from the wood of Christ's cross. Thou shalt not sink; hold thyself fast to Christ.

St Augustine, *Commentary on Psalms*

Suffering man, loving God

The very least and the very greatest sorrows that God ever suffers to befall thee, proceed from the depths of his indescribable love; and such great love were better for thee than the highest and best gifts besides that he has given thee, or ever could give thee, if thou couldst but see it in this light. So that if your little finger only aches, if you are cold, if you are hungry or thirsty, if others vex you by their words or deeds, or whatever happens to you that causes you distress or pain, it will all help to fit you for a noble and blessed state.

Johann Tauler, *Sermons*

Why should I start at the plough of the Lord, that maketh deep furrows in my soul? I know he is no idle husbandman, he purposeth a crop.

Samuel Rutherford, *Apologetical Exercitations for Divine Grace*

The most perfect peace

The most perfect peace we can attain in this miserable life consists rather in meek and patient suffering, than in an exemption from adversity; and he who has most learnt to suffer will certainly possess the greatest share of peace. He is the conqueror of himself, the lord of the world, the friend of Christ, and the heir of heaven.

The Imitation of Christ, ascribed to Thomas à Kempis

By sufferings only can we know
The nature of the life we live;
The temper of our souls they show,
How true, how pure, the love we give.
To leave my love in doubt would be
No less disgrace than misery!

I welcome, then, with heart sincere,
The cross my Saviour bids me take;
No load, no trial, is severe,
That's borne or suffered for His sake:
And thus my sorrow shall proclaim
A love that's worthy of the name.

Madame Guyon

Drink Christ

Your cup that inebriates, how splendid it is! (Psalm 22:5, Vulgate)

Drink Christ, for he is the vine.
Drink Christ, for he is the rock from which water gushed.
Drink Christ, for he is the river whose current brings joy to the city of God.
Drink Christ, for he is peace.
Drink Christ, for streams of living water flow from his body.
Drink Christ, and drink the blood by which you are redeemed.
Drink Christ and drink his words.

St Ambrose, *Commentary on Psalms*

Beams of love

O thou great Power, in whom I move,
For whom I live, to whom I die,
Behold me through thy beams of love,
Whilst on this couch of tears I lie,
    And cleanse my sordid soul within
    By thy Christ's blood, the bath of sin.

No hallowed oils, no grains I need,
No rags of saints, no purging fire,
One rosy drop from David's seed
Was worlds of seas to quench thine ire.
    O precious ransom, which once paid
    That Consummatum Est was said:

And said by him that said no more,
But sealed it with his sacred breath.
Thou then, that hast dispunged my score,
And dying was the death of Death,
    Be to me now – on thee I call –
    My Life, my Strength, my Joy, my All.

Sir Henry Wotton, *A hymn to my God in the night of my late sickness*

Strength to endure

To the Reverend Mother N.

I do not ask God that you should be delivered from your sufferings, but I never cease to ask him to give you the strength and patience to endure them for as long as he sees fit. Find consolation in him who keeps you nailed to the cross. He will free you from it when he thinks that it is right. Happy are they who suffer for him. Grow accustomed thus to suffer. Ask him for strength to suffer all that which he wills, and for as long as he shall judge it to be needful for you. The world does not comprehend these truths, and I am not surprised. They suffer like people of the world but not as Christians. They think of sickness as Nature's afflictions, and not as signs of God's grace. That is why they only find there what is hostile and rough in Nature. But people who look on them as coming from God's hand, as a result of his mercy, and as the means which he uses for their salvation, commonly find in them great happiness and real consolation.

Brother Lawrence, *The Practice of the Presence of God*

PART SEVEN

OLD AGE AND DYING

In my Father's house are many rooms;
if it were not so, I would have told you.
I am going there to prepare a place for you.
(John 14:2)

An inordinate fear of death

To a penitent (April 7, 1617)
I am laying before you a few thoughts which, if you reflect on
them, may lessen that fear of death which terrifies you so much
when you are ill or with child.

First of all, I assure you that if you persevere in a life given
to serving God, as you are doing, you will find that the fear of
death will gradually ease. As your soul steers clear of harmful
emotions and becomes more firmly fixed in God, you will
notice yourself setting less store on this mortal existence and its
stupid pleasures.

Secondly, frequently fill your mind with thoughts of the
great gentleness and mercy with which God our Saviour wel-
comes souls at death, if they have spent their lives trusting in
him. 'Surely God is good . . . to those who are pure in heart'
(Psalm 73:1).

Thirdly, often lift up your heart towards our Redeemer in
holy confidence mingled with profound humility, as if to say:
I am wretched, Lord, but you will take my wretchedness and
lay it in the heart of your mercy, and lead me by your fatherly
hand into the joy of your inheritance. Weak, abject and poor as
I am, in that moment you will look on me with love, for I have
hoped in you and desired to be all yours.

St François de Sales, *An Introduction to the Devout Life*

The benefits of looking death in the face

It is a good thing to go down to the gates of death. We can see God more closely there and we become used to what must happen to us before long. One should learn about oneself from drawing so near to God's judgment and to his eternal truth.

Use this grace so that you can become more detached from the world and even more detached from yourself. We cling to all outer things for the sake of ourselves, and all other attachments can be traced back to this. Love God and renounce yourself out of love for him.

Do not cling to your own talents and strength. Do not indulge in self-complacency as you use God's gifts of sincerity and generosity towards other people. All these do not come from God but they all turn to poison and only puff up our pride as soon as we secretly put our trust in them. We need to be nothing in our own eyes and to act as if this were really true. We should spend our whole lives as if we were in hiding, as if we did not exist, just as our dear Lord hides himself in the sacrament of his love.

François Fénelon, *Christian Perfection*

Facing death

God be in my head
God be in my head, and in my understanding;
God be in mine eyes, and in my looking;
God be in my mouth, and in my speaking;
God be in my heart, and in my thinking;
God be at my end, and at my departing.

Horae B.V.M. (Sarum) 1514

Meditating on death

Life soon passeth away.

Oh the stupidity and hardness of the human heart, that thinks only about the present, and does not sufficiently regard the future. In every thought, and every action, you should hold yourself in readiness as if you were to die today.

Do not let the examples of your friends and neighbours, nor any confidence in their wisdom, make you defer the care of your salvation to a future time.

Live in the world as a stranger and pilgrim, who has no concern with its business or pleasures; and knowing that you have no abiding city here, keep your heart disentangled from earthly passions, and lifted up to God. There let your daily prayers, and sighs, and tears, be directed; that, after death, your spirit may be happily wafted to heaven.

The Imitation of Christ, ascribed to Thomas à Kempis

Live in Christ, live in Christ, and the flesh need not fear death.

John Knox's dying words

On death

O death, why do you delay?
Why come so slowly to the living yet mortal?
Why do you not embrace the one who desires you?
Who can assess the measure of sweetness which ends sighs and
begins the blessings,
The gate to unfailing joy and all that can be desired?
Look, I sigh; I long for you!
Come, and I shall be saved.
Ravished with love,
I cannot fully enjoy my desire,
Till you give me the joy I must taste.
I must pass through your path,
As did my fathers.
I beg you not to delay;
Do not keep me at bay-
See how I pine for love;
How I long to die;
How I am on fire for you!
But come quickly, not for your sake,
But on account of the Saviour's, Jesus,
Upon whom, there, I shall gaze eternally.
Death, how good is your sentence,
On needy man, whose soul
Is sweetened by love;
For the contemplative who truly loves Christ,
Sweetly aflame with love's fire.
Richard Rolle, *The Fire of Love*

Facing death in old age

Death becomes a reality when you contemplate it in solitude and in old age.

We have to face our end even though it is totally repugnant to our nature. M. Olier, shortly before his death, used to take up his own hand and say, 'Body of sin, you will soon go to corruption. O eternity you are indeed very near to me!'

It is not a question of rejoicing at the prospect of death, as such joy does not depend on ourselves and many great saints have not experienced it. Let us be satisfied with what does depend on our own free will as it is upheld and strengthened by God's grace. As we do this we shall not be listening to the promptings of nature but we shall be wholeheartedly accepting what we are unable to rejoice in.

Nature shrinks from drinking the bitter cup of death. However, our inner being can say with our dear Lord: 'My Father, if it is possible, may this cup be taken from me. Yet not as I will, but as you will' (Matthew 26:39).

St Francis de Sales makes the distinction between consent and feeling. We are not masters of our own feelings but we are, by God's grace, masters of giving consent to our feelings.

Wait patiently for death to come and do not think about it in a sad way. Ignore man's forgetfulness and remember the one true, divine Friend who will never forget you.

François Fénelon, *Letters*

We have a good master

As St Ambrose was dying he was asked by those around him if he was not taken up with fear of God's judgments. He only answered, 'We have a good Master.' And this is what we should say to ourselves. It is necessary, as St Augustine says, that we are reduced to the point of having nothing to offer God except for our own misery and God's mercy. Our misery is the reason God has mercy on us and God's mercy is our only source of strength.

When we are depressed, read whatever is best suited to foster trust and books that will comfort your heart. 'Surely God is good to Israel, to those who are pure in heart' (Psalm 73:1). Ask God to give you that pure heart he so much wants you to have and which makes him so compassionate towards our infirmities.

François Fénelon, *Christian Perfection*

To a lady in sickness

I hear, my dear daughter, that you are ill, and I am deeply sorry about this, although I shall do nothing except what God wills, either for you or for myself. I am sure that you will readily submit yourself and that, when you realise that you are unable to give God anything, you will allow him to take whatever he wills.

We give back to someone only what we received in the first place. You should not regard anything in this world as yours. A servant allows his master to reclaim anything that has been entrusted to him. You should apply this to your human life. 'Though I constantly take my life in my hands, I will not forget your law' (Psalm 119:109). Allow your life to pass into God's hands because he knows how best to deal with you. '. . . Your life is now hidden with Christ in God' (Colossians 3:3) is never more true than when we die to the unreal life of this world.

The true life is unknown to and cannot be understood by the foolish world. Many people who want to be wise and who are semi-religious do not want themselves to be detached from life by God's hand, as they come face to face with death. Other people think a great deal about death without considering how they have to die to themselves. This is the only way people can become indifferent to physical death, even when they are not specifically thinking about death. We can only become fit for physical death if we die to everything else first.

François Fénelon, *Letters*

Face to face with death

Son, for mine own part I have no further delight in anything in this life. What I do here any longer, and to what end I am here, I know not. Now my wishes are accomplished. One thing there was, for which I desired to linger for a while in this life, that I might see thee a Catholic Christian before I died. My God hath done this for me abundantly, that I should now see thee withal despising earthly happiness and become his servant: what do I here?

St Augustine, *Confessions* (words of his mother, Monica)

This is the mental attitude in which it is not hard to die. Self-love is unreal love; the love of God is our only true life: so as the last expels the first everything is safe. There is no life except in this happy death. 'Therefore,' as St Paul writes, 'we do not lose heart. Though outwardly we are wasting away, yet inwardly we are being renewed day by day' (2 Corinthians 4:16).

Let God alone reign in your heart. Let him smash the idol 'I'. Be completely absorbed by God as you have been by 'I'. Sacrifice that 'I' to God and then you will find peace, freedom and life, in spite of pain, weakness and death itself.

François Fénelon, *Christian Perfection*

Death, be not proud

Death, be not proud, though some have called thee
Mighty and dreadful, for thou art not so:
For those whom thou think'st thou dost overthrow
Die not, poor Death; nor yet canst thou kill me.
From Rest and Sleep, which but thy picture be,
Much pleasure, then from thee much more must flow;
And soonest our best men with thee do go –
Rest of their bones and souls' delivery!
Thou'rt slave to fate, chance, kings, and desperate men,
And dost with poison, war, and sickness dwell;
And poppy or charms can make us sleep as well
And better than thy stroke. Why swell'st thou then?
One short sleep past, we wake eternally,
And Death shall be no more: Death, thou shalt die!

John Donne

Dying well

Jesus called out with a loud voice, 'Father, into your hands I commit my spirit.' When he had said this, he breathed his last (Luke 23:46).

A true Christian, who has control over his own will, may live nobly and happily, and enjoy a clear heaven within the serenity of his own mind perpetually. When the sea of this world is most rough and tempestuous about him, then can he ride safely at anchor within the haven, by a sweet compliance of his will to God's will. He can look about him, and with an even and indifferent mind behold the world either to smile or frown upon him; neither will he abate of the least of his contentment for all the unkindness he meets in this life.

He who has mastery over his own will feels no violence from without, finds no contests within; and when God calls for him out of this state of mortality, he finds in himself a power to lay down his own life; neither is it so much taken from him, as quietly and freely surrendered up by him.

John Smith, *Exercitations for Divine Love*

Dying, let me still abide

Jesu, grant me this, I pray,
Ever in thy heart to stay;
Let me evermore abide
Hidden in thy wounded side.

If the evil one prepare,
Or the world, a tempting snare,
I am safe when I abide
In thy heart and wounded side.

If the flesh, more dangerous still,
Tempt my soul to deeds of ill,
Naught I fear when I abide
In thy heart and wounded side.

Death will come one day to me;
Jesu, cast me not from thee:
Dying let me still abide
In thy heart and wounded side.

Latin, 17th century, translated by H. W. Baker

Dying

While I draw this fleeting breath,
When mine eyes are closed in death,
When I soar through tracts unknown,
See thee on thy judgement throne;
Rock of ages, cleft for me,
Let me hide myself in thee.

Augustus Toplady

Whether I live or die

Lord, it belongs not to my care
Whether I die or live;
To love and serve Thee is my share,
And this Thy grace must give.

If life be long, I will be glad,
That I may long obey;
If short, yet why should I be sad
To soar to endless day?

Christ leads me through no darker rooms
Than he went through before,
He that into God's kingdom comes
Must enter by this door.

Richard Baxter

Last words

No coward soul is mine,
No trembler in the world's storm-troubled sphere:
   I see Heaven's glories shine,
And faith shines equal, arming me from fear.

O God within my breast,
Almighty, ever-present Deity!
   Life – that in me has rest,
As I – undying Life – have power in Thee!

Though earth and man were gone,
And suns and universe cease to be,
   And thou wert left alone,
Every existence would exist in thee.

There is not room for Death,
Nor atom that his might could render void;
   Thou – thou art Being and Breath,
And what thou art may never be destroyed.

Emily Brontë's last lines before her death

Abide with me

Abide with me; fast falls the eventide;
The darkness deepens; Lord, with me abide!
When other helpers fail, and comforts flee,
Help of the helpless, O abide with me.

Swift to its close ebbs out life's little day;
Earth's joys grow dim, its glories pass away;
Change and decay in all around I see;
O thou who changest not, abide with me.

I need thy presence every passing hour;
What but thy grace can foil the tempter's power?
Who like thyself my guide and stay can be?
Through cloud and sunshine, O abide with me.

I fear no foe with thee at hand to bless;
Ills have no weight, and tears no bitterness.
Where is death's sting? where, grave, thy victory?
I triumph still, if thou abide with me.

Hold thou thy cross before my closing eyes;
Shine through the gloom, and point me to the skies:
Heaven's morning breaks, and earth's vain shadows flee;
In life, in death, O Lord, abide with me!
H. F. Lyte

PART EIGHT

BEREAVEMENT

*After that, we who are still alive and are left
will be caught up together with them in the clouds
to meet the Lord in the air.
And so we will be with the Lord for ever.
(1 Thessalonians 4:17)*

On the death of your husband

It is a slight consolation to tell you that I sympathise deeply with your grief, but this is all human friends can do for you, as you have to turn to God for everything else. And indeed, Madame, I do turn with my whole heart to the Comforter of the afflicted and the strength of the weak.

I do not pray that God will take away your grief but that he will transform it so that you may benefit from it, and so, not overwhelm you. When God parts two people, who have been united in the most sacred bonds, he is sending a blessing on them both. God takes the first person into his own eternal glory, and through his healing sorrow he saves the second person who is left for a short time in this world.

François Fénelon, *Letters*

Accept sorrow

Ah, if you knew what peace there is in an accepted sorrow!

Madame Guyon, *A Short and Easy Method of Prayer*

Christians in their sorrows

Great sorrow is the sovereign remedy for the most dangerous evil of our nature, for in the middle of such sorrow, the central mystery of Christianity, the inner crucifixion of the natural man, takes place. Then all the powerful work of grace is achieved as self is rooted out. If this does not happen the love of God does not reign in us. We must leave the self behind before we can give ourselves to God. To jolt us out of ourselves some severe wound to our heart is needed so that everything in the world is turned to bitterness. Then the heart, wounded at its most tender place, torn from its most loved moorings, realises that it can find no rest within itself and so it goes outside itself and throws itself on God.

This is the cure for the serious sicknesses with which sin overwhelms us. The cure seems to be drastic but the disease is very deep-seated. This is what really supports Christians in their sorrows.

François Fénelon, *Letters*

Your days of grief will come to an end. I, the Lord, will be your eternal light, more lasting than the sun and moon.
Isaiah 60:20, GNB

The death of the Marquis de Crevecoeur

To Nicolas de Harlai de Bonneuil
On the death of his son-in-law

November 12th, 1701

I wish that I could be with you in order to share your grief and
endeavour to comfort you. But you know where true comfort
comes from for all those who have lost loved ones. Christianity
can give no better comfort than to tell us that we have not lost
them for ever, and that there is a home to which we are daily
drawing nearer, in which we shall all meet again. So let us not
sorrow like people who have no hope. I am deprivèd of the
pleasure of seeing you, but I remember how speedily life goes
by, and I hope that before long we shall meet for ever in God.
People who die with this faith are only absent for a few years,
or maybe only a few months. Their apparent loss should help
us to loosen our grip on the world, where we must lose everything, and draw us to the world, where we shall find everything
again.

. . . God only ever strikes us out of love and he never takes
anything away from us except to return it to us. I pray that God
may comfort you, preserve your health and completely turn
your heart to him. Happy is the person who lives by faith,
trusts in no one else except God and lives in this world as if he
had already gone beyond it.

François Fénelon, *Letters*

Passionate grief does not link us with the dead, but cuts us off
from them.

C. S. Lewis, *A Grief Observed* (written after his wife died of cancer)

The tearless life

Brief life is here our portion,
Brief sorrow, short-lived care;
The life that knows no ending,
The tearless life is there.

There grief is turned to pleasure,
Such pleasure as below
No human voice can utter,
No human heart can know.

For he whom now we trust in
Shall then be seen and known,
And they that know and see him,
Shall have him for their own.

The morning shall awaken,
The shadows shall decay,
And each true-hearted servant
Shall shine as doth the day.

Then all the halls of Sion
For ay shall be complete,
And in the Land of Beauty,
All things of beauty meet.

Bernard of Cluny, translated by J. M. Neale

No more tears

[God] will wipe every tear from their eyes. There will be no more death or mourning or crying or pain, for the old order of things has passed away.

Revelation 21:4

PART NINE

THE HOPE OF HEAVEN

*I tell you the truth,
he who believes
has everlasting life.
(John 6:47)*

The hope of heaven

To Ernest, Bishop of Rochester (1076)

When I learn that your body is worn out by fierce and incessant pain that brings you almost to the point of death, the news saddens me and humanly speaking fills me with grief. However, the thought that this is precisely the way your soul is being made ripe for eternity refreshes me and I watch your growth in holiness with spiritual happiness.

Your reverence is surely well aware that afflictions and the suffering of the body burn away the rust of sin and perfect the life of the just. Holy Scripture assures us that God scourges every son whom he receives (see Hebrews 12:6); it tells us further that tribulation brings endurance, and endurance brings character, and character brings hope, and hope does not disappoint us (see Romans 5:3–4).

This teaches us beyond all doubt that we will find joy in suffering in proportion as we have lived in hope and as we have laboured for the perfection of our inheritance as sons of God.

St Anselm, *Letters*

Our last awakening

Bring us, O Lord God, at our last awakening into the house and gate of heaven, to enter that gate and dwell in that house, where there shall be no darkness nor dazzling, but one equal light; no noise nor silence, but one equal music; no fears nor hopes, but one equal possession; no ends nor beginnings, but one equal eternity; in the habitations of thy glory and dominion, world without end.

John Donne, *Progress of the Soul*

The beatific vision

We shall rest and we shall see, we shall see and we shall love, we shall love and we shall praise. Behold what shall be in the end without end. For what else is our end except to reach the kingdom which has no end?

St Augustine, *The City of God*

For ever with the Lord!

For ever with the Lord!
Amen; so let it be:
Life from the dead is in that word,
'Tis immortality.
Here in the body pent,
Absent from him I roam,
Yet nightly pitch my moving tent
A day's march nearer home.

So when my latest breath
Shall rend the veil in twain,
By death I shall escape from death
And life eternal gain.
Knowing as I am known,
How shall I love that word,
And oft repeat before the throne:
For ever with the Lord!

James Montgomery

Think of –
Stepping on shore, and finding it heaven!
Of taking hold of a hand, and finding it God's hand;
Of breathing a new air, and finding it celestial air;
Of feeling invigorated, and finding it immortality;
Of passing from storm and tempest to an unbroken calm;
Of waking up, and finding it home.

Anonymous

BIOGRAPHICAL NOTES

Alfred the Great (849–899), King of Wessex

St **Ambrose** (340?–397), Bishop of Milan; composer and hymn-writer

St **Anselm** (1033?–1109), Archbishop of Canterbury

St **Augustine** (354–430), Bishop of Hippo in North Africa

H. W. Baker (1821–1877), English clergyman and hymn-writer

Richard Baxter (1615–1691), English Puritan minister and religious writer

St **Bernard** (1090–1153), Abbot of Clairvaux who wrote a monastic Rule and several mystical treatises

Bernard of Cluny (12th century), monk who wrote a poem on which is based the hymn 'Jerusalem the Golden'

Jakob Boehme (1575–1624), German mystic

Emily Brontë (1818–1848), English poet and novelist

William Cowper (1731–1800), English poet

Charles de Foucauld (1858–1916), French explorer and hermit-priest

Meister Eckhart (1260?–1327), German mystic and Dominican preacher

François Fénelon (1651–1715), Archbishop of Cambrai who wrote many letters of spiritual guidance

George Fox (1642–1691), English preacher who founded the Quaker movement

St **François de Sales** (1567–1622), Bishop of Geneva and opponent of Calvin

Madame **Guyon** (1648–1717), French Quietist author

George Herbert (1593–1633), English clergyman and poet

St **John of Avila** (1500–1569), Spanish mystic and preacher

John of Ruysbroeck (1293–1381), Flemish Augustinian mystic

St **John of the Cross** (1542–1591), Spanish mystic

John Knox (1513–1572), Scottish Reformer

William Law (1686–1761), English clergyman and spiritual adviser

Brother **Lawrence** (1605–1691), French Carmelite lay brother and mystic

C. S. Lewis (1898–1963), English literary critic and Christian writer

Martin Luther (1483–1546), German Reformer

H. F. Lyte (1793–1847), English clergyman

George Macdonald (1824–1905), Scottish congregational minister and Christian writer

James Montgomery (1771–1854), Scottish poet

J. M. Neale (1818–1866), English translator of Latin and Greek hymns

Cardinal **J. H. Newman** (1801–1890), English Tractarian who later converted to Roman Catholicism

John Newton (1725–1807), English evangelical clergyman and hymn-writer

St **Patrick** (5th century), English missionary in Ireland

Richard Rolle (1300?–1349), English mystic

Christina G. Rossetti (1830–1894), English poet

Samuel Rutherford (1600?–1661), Scottish Presbyterian minister

Lord **Shaftesbury** (1801–1885), English politician and social reformer

William Shakespeare (1564–1616), English dramatist

Dr **John Smith** (1618–1652), Cambridge Platonist

C. H. Spurgeon (1834–1892), English Baptist minister

Johann Tauler (1300–1361), German mystic and Dominican, successor to Eckhart

Jeremy Taylor (1613–1667), Anglican Bishop of Down and Connor

St **Teresa of Avila** (1515–1582), Spanish Carmelite mystic

Thomas à Kempis (1380?–1471), German devotional theologian who probably wrote *The Imitation of Christ*

Augustus Toplady (1740–1778), English clergyman and hymn-writer

Isaac Watts (1674–1748), English hymn-writer

John Wesley (1703–1791), English clergyman, founder of Methodism

Sir **Henry Wotton** (1568–1639), English diplomat and poet